JOURNAL

With A Crash And A BANG!

Senior Author
John J. Pikulski

Senior Coordinating Author
J. David Cooper

Senior Consulting Author
William K. Durr

Coordinating Authors
Kathryn H. Au
M. Jean Greenlaw
Marjorie Y. Lipson
Susan E. Page
Sheila W. Valencia
Karen K. Wixson

Authors
Rosalinda B. Barrera
Edwina Bradley
Ruth P. Bunyan
Jacqueline L. Chaparro
Jacqueline C. Comas
Alan N. Crawford
Robert L. Hillerich
Timothy G. Johnson
Jana M. Mason
Pamela A. Mason
William E. Nagy
Joseph S. Renzulli
Alfredo Schifini

Senior Advisor
Richard C. Anderson

Advisors
Christopher J. Baker
Charles Peters
MaryEllen Vogt

HOUGHTON MIFFLIN COMPANY   BOSTON
Atlanta   Dallas   Geneva, Illinois   Palo Alto   Princeton   Toronto

Printed in the U.S.A.

ISBN: 0-395-61965-3

3456789-B-96 95 94 93

CONTENTS

THEME 1: Surprise!

THEME 2: Scared Silly

CONTENTS

SURPRISE!

A Surprise for You!

Name _____

Date _____

More Surprises!

✳ Read stories about surprises.

✳ Learn about the order of events in a story and the feelings of its characters.

✳ Choose books and writing projects that interest you.

✳ Make a Surprise Scrapbook.

✳ Write a class story and other stories about surprises.

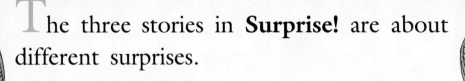

The three stories in **Surprise!** are about different surprises.

Look at the pictures in these stories. What do you think each story is about?

_____

_____

1._____

_____

_____

2._____

_____

_____

3._____

Which story do you think will have the most surprises for you? Why? Make a mark in the box.

1. <u>This Is the Bear</u>   ☐
2. <u>Fix-It</u>   ☐
3. <u>Do Like Kyla</u>   ☐

Draw a picture of what you think one of the surprises is.

This Is the Bear

This story has a surprise.
What do you think the surprise will be?
Draw your idea.

Share your picture with a friend.

Responding to the Literature

What part of the story did you like best? Draw it here.

Tell why you liked this part best.

_____

_____

_____

_____

_____

_____

4 *Theme 1 Surprise!* THIS IS THE BEAR

Developing Skills Through Literature

Sequence

Think about <u>This</u> <u>Is</u> <u>the</u> <u>Bear</u>.
For each pair of sentences below, write **1** to show
what happens first and **2** to show what happens next.

_____ The man takes the bear to the dump.

_____ The dog pushes the bear into the bin.

_____ The boy takes the bus to the dump.

_____ The man and the boy look in the dump for the bear.

_____ The man drives the boy, the bear, and the dog home.

_____ The dog finds the bear at the dump.

What was the surprise ending?

_____

_____

_____

_____

_____

_____

Characters' Feelings

Draw a picture of a character from <u>This Is the</u> <u>Bear</u> to answer each question. Then write who the picture shows.

1. Who was cold and cross?

   _____

   _____

   _____

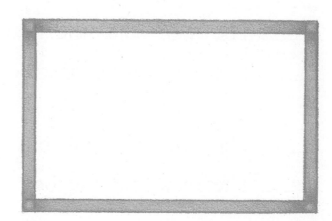

2. Who was in a grump?

   _____

   _____

   _____

3. Who was surprised at the end?

   _____

   _____

   _____

Exploring and Extending

This Is MY Bear!

You can make your own teddy bear.
Here is what you'll need.

2 cloth bear shapes   **glue**   **filling**   **buttons**   **marker**

Here is what to do.

1. Glue the edges of the two bear shapes together. Leave one side open.

3. Glue the opening closed.

2. Put stuffing in the opening.

4. Draw a nose and a mouth with a marker. Glue on button eyes.

This Is the Bear

Draw a picture of one of your toy animals.

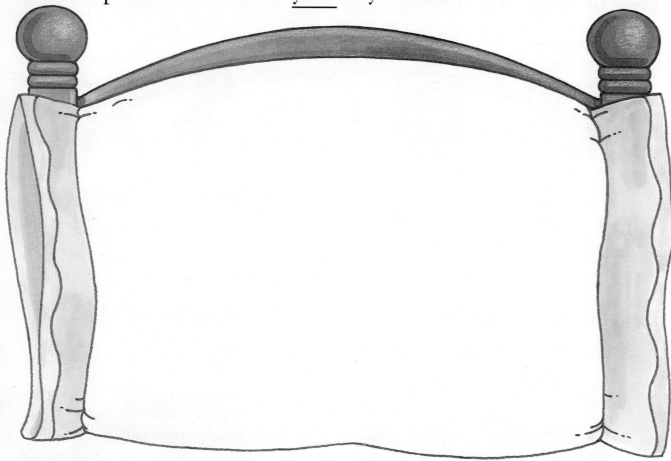

Now tell something about your toy.
Use the pattern of words from the story.
Your words do not have to rhyme.

_____

_____

This is the_____

_____

_____

that _____ .

Short <u>o</u>

The bear saw many things at the dump.
On the tags, write the names of the things he saw.

| cot | top | pot | clock | sock |

Tell about which thing you would like to find.

_____

_____

_____

Exploring and Extending

Thanks a Lot

Pretend you are the boy.
Write a note to the man at the dump.
Thank him for his help.

Dear Man,

Yours truly,

This Is the Bear

Write some words you want to remember.
Then color in and cut out the shape.

Long o

In the story, the lost bear is found at the dump.
See if you can find some other lost things there.

a broken stove   **a piece of rope**   **a garden hose**
a bent pole   **a rose bush**   **a blue robe**

Which of the things you found could be fixed?
How would you fix it?

_____

_____

_____

_____

_____

Work-a-Word Game

You can get from <u>bone</u> to <u>cape</u> by changing one letter at a time. Here's how:

bone

_____ **cone**   changed the <u>b</u> to a <u>c</u>

_____ **cane**   changed the <u>o</u> to an <u>a</u>

_____ **cape**   changed the <u>n</u> to a <u>p</u>

Now you can do it.

Change one letter at a time in the words below.

bin   **dog**

_____   _____

_____   _____

_____   _____

_____   _____

_____   _____

_____   _____

Show your first and last words to a friend. Ask if your friend can figure out what letters you changed each time.

Fix-It

In the story, a TV is broken.
How would you feel if your TV broke?

_____

_____

_____

_____

_____

Draw a picture to show what you would do.

Developing Vocabulary

Read what each person says.
Then finish each sentence.

"The TV won't work.
Please come to fix it right away."

Mother wants someone to

_____

_____

_____

_____

_____.

"I'm busy right now.
I'll come when I've finished here."

The fix-it man is

_____

_____

_____.

He will come

_____

_____

_____

_____

_____.

"Please go play in your room until the TV is fixed."

The girl will

_____

_____

_____

_____

_____.

"I've tried my best. I can't fix it. You need a new TV."

Finally the fix-it man said,

_____

_____

_____

_____

_____

_____.

What do you like to do more than watching TV?

Draw a picture. Then write about it.

_____

_____

_____

_____

_____

How to Hide a Polar Bear

Think of another animal. Draw a picture of where the animal lives. Show how it blends in with where it lives.

Now write about the animal.

_____

_____

_____

_____

_____

Sequence/Characters' Feelings

Think about what happened in the story.
Number the sentences **1, 2,** and **3** to show
what the characters did first, next, and last.

_____ Emma's mother and father
tried to fix the TV.

_____ Emma wanted to watch TV,
but it was broken.

_____ The fix-it man couldn't fix the TV.

These things made Emma feel sad.
Draw a picture to show what made Emma happy.

Compare your picture to a friend's. Did you draw
the same thing?

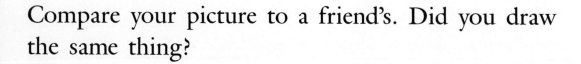

CVC Base Words and Endings

These sentences retell the story as Emma might tell it.
Add a word to the ending in each blank.
Then read the story to a friend.

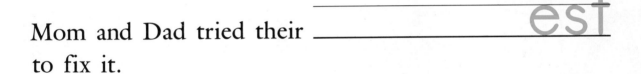

hard   read   call   want   final

I _____ ed to watch TV,
but it was broken.

Mom and Dad tried their _____ est
to fix it.

Then Dad _____ ed the fix-it man.

_____ ly, Dad fixed the TV.

But by then, I was _____ ing a book.

Fix It, Please!

What are these people fixing?

Talk about the picture with a friend.
Then draw a picture of a worker who has
helped fix something at your house.

Do Like Kyla

Think about something you have learned to do by watching someone.

Draw a picture about it.

Write the name of the person who showed you.

_____

_____

Show your picture to this person.

Developing Vocabulary

Choose one of the words in the box to complete each sentence.

| kitchen   beautiful   braids |

I think my sister

_____

_____

is _____ .

No, really. I like the way

_____

_____

she _____ her hair.

Sometimes she gets me cookies from

_____

_____

the jar in the _____ .

In Do Like Kyla, the girl telling the story wants to be just like her big sister. Is there someone you want to be like? Draw a picture of you and that person.

Write why you want to be more like that person.

_____

_____

_____

_____

_____

_____

Sequence/Characters' Feelings

In the story, the sisters go to the store together. Write the number **1, 2,** or **3** in front of each sentence to show the order of the things that happened.

_____ We crunch in the snow.

_____ We put on coats.

_____ We skip past the big store window.

Do you think Kyla likes having her little sister follow her to the store? Why? Be ready to talk about your ideas.

Compound Words

Kyla made <u>footsteps</u> in the snow.
<u>Footsteps</u> is a compound word made from
two smaller words put together.

footsteps 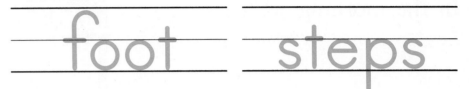 foot   steps

Each word in the box is a compound word.
Write the two smaller words on the lines.

snowman	_____	_____
	_____	_____
sunshine	_____	_____
	_____	_____
overcoat	_____	_____

What other words like these do you know?
Make a list of these words with
some friends.

The Whole Day Long

How would you spend a whole day with a sister
or a brother? Plan your day on the lines below.
Draw a picture of what you would like to do most.

In the morning we'll

_____

_____

_____

_____

_____ .

In the afternoon we'll

_____

_____

_____

_____

_____ .

After dark we'll

_____

_____

_____

_____

_____ .

A Theme PROJECT

Make a Surprise Scrapbook

Choosing and Planning

You can surprise someone, <u>or</u> you can be surprised by someone or something. To share both kinds of surprises you can

- talk about surprises
- find or make surprise pictures
- write something surprising
- put surprise ideas in a class scrapbook
- plan ways to show the surprise scrapbook

A scrapbook is a book for keeping pictures and written things in. Do you see any surprises on this page that might go in a scrapbook?

MAGIC

What kind of surprise will <u>you</u> add to the surprise scrapbook?

☐ I want to tell about a surprising book.

☐ I want to cut out pictures from a newspaper or magazine.

☐ I want to draw a surprise picture.

☐ I want to write a surprise story.

☐ I want to make up a joke.

Newspapers and magazines have pictures and stories in them. They tell about things that have happened.

Putting It Together

What do you need to help you make your scrapbook?

- ☐ writing paper
- ☐ drawing paper
- ☐ pencil
- ☐ crayons
- ☐ paper punch
- ☐ large, heavy paper for scrapbook pages

- ☐ paste
- ☐ tape
- ☐ scissors
- ☐ yarn or ribbon

_____

_____

_____

Follow these steps to make your surprise scrapbook:

1. Make neat copies of what you write.

2. Cut pictures or other pieces so they will fit on the scrapbook pages.

3. Paste or tape each of your surprises onto a page for the scrapbook.

4. Write your name at the bottom of each of your pages.

5. Work with others to put your pages together.

Now you have one big surprise scrapbook.

Presenting the Project

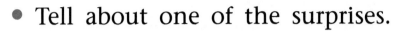

How can you and your class share the scrapbook? Here are some ideas:

- Tell about one of the surprises.
- Read a joke out loud.
- Put on a play about one of the surprises.
- Have a Silly Surprises Day. Bring in funny surprises and share the scrapbook.

Checkpoint

My surprises are

_____

_____

_____.

My idea for sharing the scrapbook is

_____

_____

_____.

Who will you and your class share your scrapbook with?

_____

_____

_____

My Own Project Plan

What kind of surprise will I make? Here
are my ideas.

_____

_____

_____

_____

What will I need to make my surprise?

_____

_____

_____

_____

How will I make my surprise? Here is my idea.

_____

_____

This is how I will share my surprise
with others.

_____

_____

_____

THE Writing Center

Writing a Story

 PREWRITING

Talking Together
Talk about some story ideas. Make a list.
Choose one idea for a story.

 PREWRITING

Drawing Our Story
Talk about what will happen at the
beginning of the story. Draw a picture.

Talk about what will happen at the
end of the story. Draw a picture.

Tell about your pictures.

Writing Our Story
Talk about the story.
Tell what you want to write.

Writing More
Read the story together.
What do you want to add?
Write more.

Sharing Our Final Copy
Write the story again.
How can you share the story?

SCARED SILLY

I Can Make You Laugh

Name _____

Date _____

You will laugh as you

❀ Read stories that are a little scary and a lot of fun

❀ Find out what things in stories can cause you to be scared and what things can cause you to laugh

❀ Choose books and writing projects that interest you

❀ Have a class Dragon Day

❀ Write about scary characters, places, and things

Who's Scared?

Draw a picture of something scary or silly. Write about your picture.

Look ahead at the stories in **Scared Silly.**

What story do you think might be scary? Why?

What story do you think might be silly? Why?

Klippity Klop

What do you think of when you
hear a klippity klop sound?
Draw a picture to show your ideas.

Get together with a friend.
Talk about your pictures.
Did you both draw the same thing?

Prince Krispin liked adventuring.
He liked being safe at home, too.
Which do you like better?
Draw a picture to show your ideas.

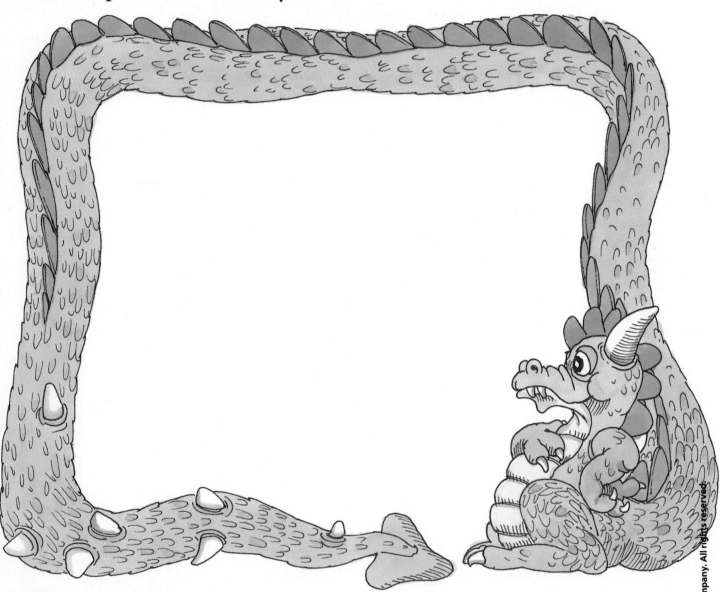

Now think of a title for your picture. Write it here.

_____

_____

_____

Cause-Effect

Prince Krispin and Dumpling came to a cave.
Suddenly, they turned and ran.
Why did they ride so fast?
Draw a picture that shows why.

Why might Prince Krispin go out riding again?
Write your ideas.

_____

_____

_____

_____

_____

Reality-Fantasy

If you went out for a ride like Prince Krispin did, what might you see?

Draw something real.   Draw something make-believe.

Write about your pictures here.

_____

_____

_____

_____

_____

Share your pictures with a friend.

Exploring and Extending

Adventuring Again

Make a map for Prince Krispin to follow the next time he goes adventuring. Cut out the pictures at the bottom of the page. Paste them onto the map. Then draw a line to show the way Prince Krispin might go.

| hill | field | cave | bridge | stream |

Klippity Klop

On Prince Krispin's ride, he rode
over, across, through, down,
and up.

Now you can plan a ride.
Think about where you will go.
Then choose an animal to ride on.
Draw your ideas here.
Then name your animal.

Follow the pattern of <u>Klippity Klop</u> as you write
about your ride. Draw pictures for
what you write.

We came to a _____
and rode over it.

We came to a _____
and rode through it.

We came to a _____
hill and rode down it.

We came to a _____
hill and rode up it.

Chinese Dragons

Now that you have read about dragons,
how do you feel about them?

_____

_____

_____

_____

_____

Draw a picture of your own face to show what it
would look like if you met a dragon.

Tell a friend about
your picture.

Short <u>u</u>

What do you think dragons eat?

_____

_____

_____

Here is a silly recipe for dragon food.
Write the letter <u>u</u> where it is missing.
Read the recipe to find out what a dragon eats.
Then draw a picture of a hungry dragon.

How to Feed a Dragon

Take a c___p of b___gs.

Add some l___mps of m___d.

Drop in a b___nch of n___ts.

Mix in soap s___ds.

Pour into a m___g.

Give to the dragon for l___nch.

Who Is Hiding Here?

Look back at the pictures in <u>Klippity Klop</u>.
What animals can you find in the fields and streams?
Add your pictures of animals to the scene below.

Ask a friend to find all your animals.

Klippity Klop

Fill this castle with words that make you think of Prince Krispin's ride back to his castle.

Write the words on the lines in the castle.

My Word Castle

Long u

Help Prince Krispin write a letter about his ride.
Write the letter u in each blank to make whole words.
Then read the letter to a friend.

Dear D___ke,

Dumpling and I went for a ride. It was a
sunny day in J___ne. As we rode, I sang a happy
t___ne.

Then we saw a h___ge dragon. The dragon
was r___de. When it saw us, it roared. We were
scared silly! We ran home as fast as we could.

Your friend,
Prince Krispin

Signs for Dragons

Here are some signs you may have seen.

Make a sign to put up near a dragon's cave.
It should tell or show that a dragon lives nearby.

The Gunnywolf

Do you think wolves are scary?
There are wolves in many stories.

Can you find the word <u>wolf</u> in the title,
The <u>Gunnywolf</u>?
Draw a picture of a wolf from a story you know,
or make up a wolf of your own.

Share your wolf pictures.

The <u>Gunnywolf</u> takes place in a deep woods. What do you think a deep woods looks like?

To make a picture of a deep woods, follow these directions. Read all the directions <u>before</u> you begin.

- Draw lots of trees. Make your woods look dark and deep.
- Draw a flower just inside the woods.
- Put the flower between two trees.

A little girl and a silly animal are in the deep, dark woods in <u>The</u> <u>Gunnywolf</u>.

Draw pictures of animals you think might be in or next to the woods. Be sure to read all the directions <u>before</u> you begin.

- Draw one tiny animal.
- Draw one animal that can run fast.
- Draw one animal that is slow.

Now write a sound one animal might make.

_____

_____

_____

What do you think? Was <u>The</u> <u>Gunnywolf</u> scary or silly?

_____

_____

_____

Draw the part of the story that you liked best.

Developing Skills Through Literature

Cause-Effect

Why did the Little Girl go into the woods?
Draw a picture that shows why.

What made the Gunnywolf fall asleep?
Write a sentence that tells.

Reality-Fantasy

The Little Girl met a make-believe creature in the woods.

Talk with a friend about some <u>real</u> things you might see in the woods.

Draw a picture of your ideas.

Now write about your picture.

_____

_____

_____

_____

_____

CVC Base Words and Endings

Add a word to each ending. Then mark <u>yes</u> or <u>no</u> to answer the questions. Remember that some words change before the ending is added.

fun	nut	loud	skip

1. Go _____ in the woods.
   Will the Gunnywolf wake up? ☐ Yes ☐ No

2. Crack _____ like a squirrel.
   Will the Gunnywolf wake up? ☐ Yes ☐ No

3. Tell _____ stories to
   the Gunnywolf. Is he awake yet? ☐ Yes ☐ No

4. Now say the ABC's _____.
   With luck, you'll wake the Gunnywolf up!

Funny Gunny Animals

The Gunnywolf was a funny kind of wolf.

Make up other funny kinds of animals.

Add the name of an animal you know to **Gunny**.

The first one is done for you.

Gunny rabbit

Gunny _____

Gunny _____

Gunny _____

Gunny _____

Gunny _____

Now draw your Funny Gunny Animals.

Work with a friend to make more Gunny animals.

Strange Bumps

In the story <u>Strange</u> <u>Bumps</u>, an Owl sees some strange bumps in his bed.

Here are some strange bumps under the covers.

What would another animal look like under the covers? Draw a picture.

Ask your friends to guess what's under the covers.

In the story, Owl is going to sleep.
Pretend that the bed in the picture is yours.
Follow the directions to finish the picture.

1. Show what you will cover yourself with.

2. Add a teddy bear at the foot of your bed.

3. Draw a sleeping pet under your bed.

4. Put a book of your own near the bed.

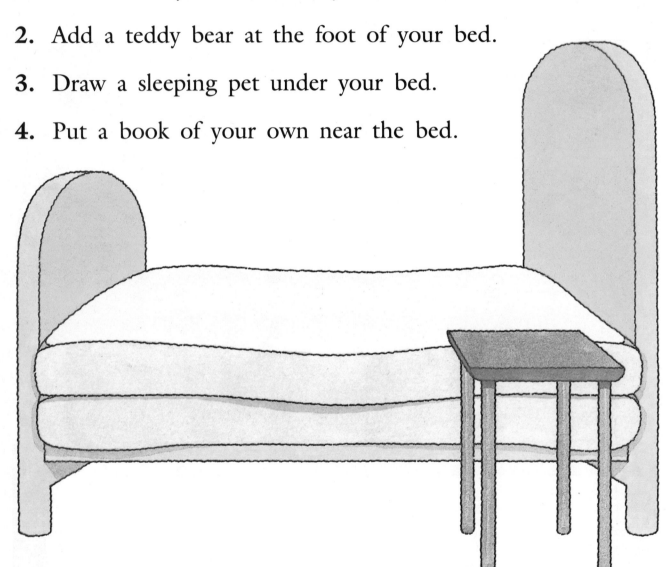

What will you dream about while you sleep?

_____

_____

_____

What do you think is the silliest part of the story?
Draw a picture. Then write about it.

_____

_____

_____

_____

_____

Developing Skills Through Literature

Cause-Effect/Reality-Fantasy

What made the bumps in Owl's bed?

Draw a picture of Owl.

Circle what made the bumps.

Now pretend that Owl has a friend to sleep over.

Draw a picture of them.

Show how many bumps they would see.

Short and Long <u>u</u>

These sentences tell about the story.

Owl was snug in bed.
Then he saw the bumps.

"This is not fun," said Owl.
Those are just lumps now.
But they might grow bigger.
They might get to be huge!"

Owl got up.
He jumped on the bed.
The bed went THUMP!

How many short <u>u</u> and long <u>u</u> words
can you find in this story?
Work with a friend to find the short <u>u</u>
and long <u>u</u> words.

_____

_____

_____

_____

_____

_____

_____

_____

Surprise Bumps

Play a guessing game with a friend.

Pick things with different sizes and shapes.
Hide something under a sheet.
Ask a friend to guess what is hiding.

You might hide a ball, a large stuffed
toy, or a book.

Write the names of the things you hid.
Put a check next to any your friend guessed.

_____

_____

_____ ☐   _____ ☐

_____

_____

_____ ☐   _____ ☐

_____

_____

_____ ☐   _____ ☐

_____

_____ ☐   _____ ☐

A Theme PROJECT

Have a Dragon Day
Choosing and Planning

Oh my! Dragons in the class? Yes! You can have a class Dragon Day!

- Find dragon pictures.
- Write or tell about dragons.
- Make a giant dragon.
- Do a dragon dance.
- Share dragon ideas.

What do you know about dragons?

_____

_____

Dragons have _____.

_____

Dragons have _____

_____

_____

_____.

What can you do for Dragon Day? Here are ideas of things to do on your own.

- ☐ Find storybooks with dragon pictures.
- ☐ Tell a dragon story.
- ☐ Make dragon art.
- ☐ Write about a dragon.

Here are ideas of things to do with a group.

- ☐ Make a big paper dragon.
- ☐ Make up a dragon dance. Use music that fits how dragons move.

Dragons can be different. Circle the kind
of dragon you like.

Will the dragon

☐ walk or fly?

☐ help or make trouble?

Is the dragon

☐ silly or scary?

☐ kind or mean?

☐ fast or slow?

Checkpoint

Here is my plan for Dragon Day.

On my own, I will

_____

_____

_____ .

_____

My group will _____

_____

_____ .

Putting It Together

Make up a dragon dance!

- Find good dragon music.
- Be one big dragon or many small dragons.
- Move like a dragon moves. Dance with the music.
- This is my dance idea.

_____

_____

_____

What will you wear to dance in?

Make a giant dragon.

- Draw a very big dragon shape.
- Dress up the dragon.

Checkpoint

I need these things.

_____

_____

_____

_____

_____

_____

Presenting the Project

How will you share your dragons?

Who would like to see the dance?

_____

_____

_____

Who would like to see the art?

_____

_____

_____

Who would like to hear the stories?

_____

_____

_____

Checkpoint

I will ask these people to come on Dragon Day.

_____

_____

_____

_____

My Own Project Plan

What can I find out? Here are some ideas.

_____

_____

_____

_____

_____

                      _____

                      _____

I will learn about _____ .

This is how I will find things out.

_____

1. _____

_____

2. _____

_____

3. _____

This is what I will make or do.

THE Writing Center

Describing a Scary Creature

PREWRITING ➤

I Can Write About...

What scary or silly creature can you write about?
Draw pictures of two creatures here.

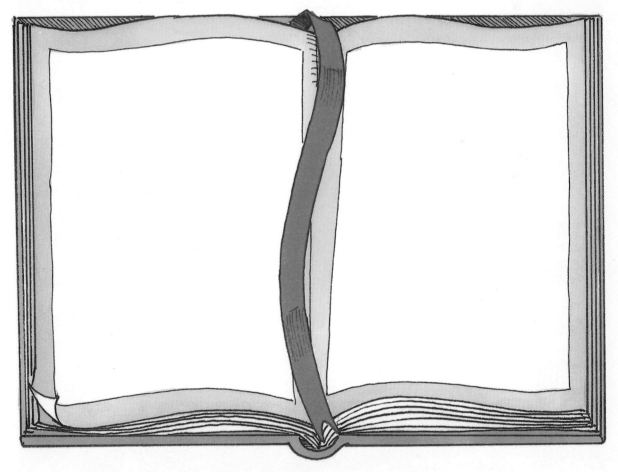

Talk about your pictures with someone.
Choose one to write about.

I Can Tell...

What can you tell about your creature?
Where does it live? What does it eat?
Does it have friends?

Draw a picture to show more about
your creature.

Now tell someone about your creature.

DRAFTING

Writing About My Creature
Look at the picture you drew.
Now write about your creature.

Writing More

Read what you wrote to someone.
Then talk about it.
Here are some things to talk about.

- Does your creature have a name?
- What color is it?
- How big is it?
- Does it have hair?

Read to yourself what you wrote.
What can you add?
Go back and write more.

Sharing Your Final Copy

Think of a title.
Copy what you wrote about your creature.
Share what you wrote with a friend.

76

78

CATS

Get ready to find out about cats.

- Read different kinds of stories about cats.

- Retell stories you have read.

- Choose books and writing projects that interest you.

- Have a class cat show.

- Write about what different cats look like and what they do.

I Belong To

Name _____

Date _____

What in the World Is a Cat?

What does this make you think of?

Draw your ideas. Then write what you know about cats.

_____

_____

_____

_____

_____

_____

_____

No One Should Have Six Cats!

Are six cats too many?
Are six cats enough?
What do you think?

_____
_____
_____
_____
_____
_____

Which of David's cats would you like to have?
Draw a picture of that cat. Write the cat's name.

Story Elements

Tell the story about David's cats.

▼ **Beginning**   What was David's problem?

_____

_____

_____

▼ **Middle**   Tell about David's six cats.

_____

1. _____

_____

_____

_____

2. _____

_____

_____

_____

3. _____

_____

_____

_____

4. _____

_____

_____

_____

5. _____

_____

_____

_____

6. _____

_____

_____

▼ **End** Tell something about cat number seven.

_____

_____

_____

_____

Now tell the story to a friend.

Wanted: A Good Home

What if David had to give away one cat?
Help David find a good home for it.
Make a poster. Use both words and pictures.

Wanted:
A Good Home For

No One Should Have Six Cats!

Pretend you are David.
Tell about cat number seven.

_____

_____

_____ is cat number seven.

_____

_____

My mother found her _____.
And nobody wanted her.
What could we do?
We had no choice.
We let her live with us.

_____

_____

Now _____

_____

_____

_____.

Short <u>e</u>

We are David's cats. He told you about us. Now use the words in the box to help us tell you about David.

pet fed mend best let bed

_____
_____

"I'm Herkie. David had to _____ my hurt paw."

_____

"I'm Zip. David _____ me live with him."

_____

"I'm Shadow. David likes to _____ me."

"I'm Tinker. David sleeps above me on

_____
_____

his _____ ."

_____

"I'm Boots. David _____ me milk."

_____

"I'm Hairy. David is a cat's _____ friend."

Caring for Pets

Think about a pet you would like to have.
Draw a picture to show what you would
do to care for it.

Write about caring for a pet.

_____

_____

_____

_____

_____

_____

No One Should Have Six Cats!

Write some words you want to remember.

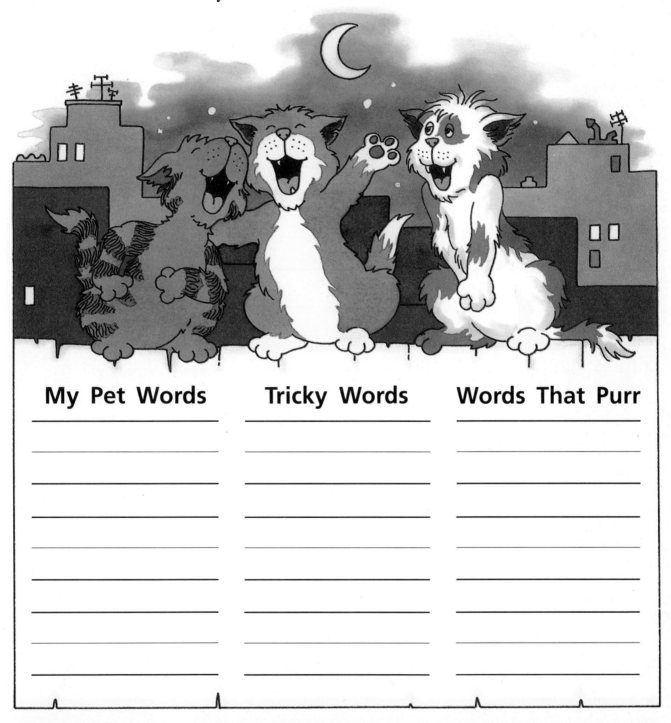

My Pet Words	Tricky Words	Words That Purr

Developing Skills

Long e

Use these pairs of rhyming words.
Help David write a poem about his cats.

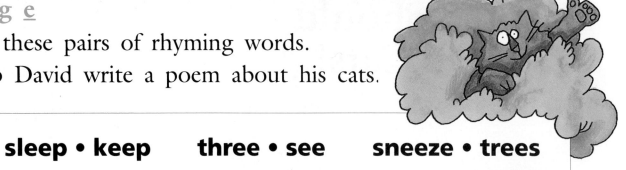

| sleep • keep | three • see | sneeze • trees |

_____

_____

Herkie likes to climb _____ .

_____

_____

Hairy makes people _____ .

_____

_____

Zip is happy to eat and _____ .

_____

_____

Tinker, my cousins couldn't _____ .

_____

_____

Shadow is cat number _____ .

_____

_____

Boots has grown, as you can _____ .

Put It on a Map

Finish this map. Add David's house.
Add his cousins' house and Belinda's house.
Show where David and his mom found their cats.

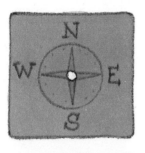

House   Cat

Ideas!

School

Playground

King Street

Mom's Office

Stores   **Bank**

Store   **Store**

Alley

Tiger Runs

Who is Tiger?

Is she a pet cat or a wild cat?

_____

_____

_____

What might make a tiger run?

Draw a picture to show your ideas.

Share your ideas with a friend.

Have you ever been in a jungle before?
Pretend that you are in a jungle now.
Draw a picture of a dangerous animal you might
see there.

Is the animal small or huge?

_____

_____

_____

What noise does the animal make?

_____

_____

_____

Talk with a friend about some other things that can happen in the jungle.

Would you feel frightened in the jungle?
Tell why.

_____

_____

_____

_____

_____

Imagine that an animal suddenly ran toward you.
Would you stay where you are? Hide? Run away?
Draw a picture to show what you would do.

In the story, an elephant scared Tiger.
What animal might scare you? Draw a picture of the animal.
Tell about your picture.

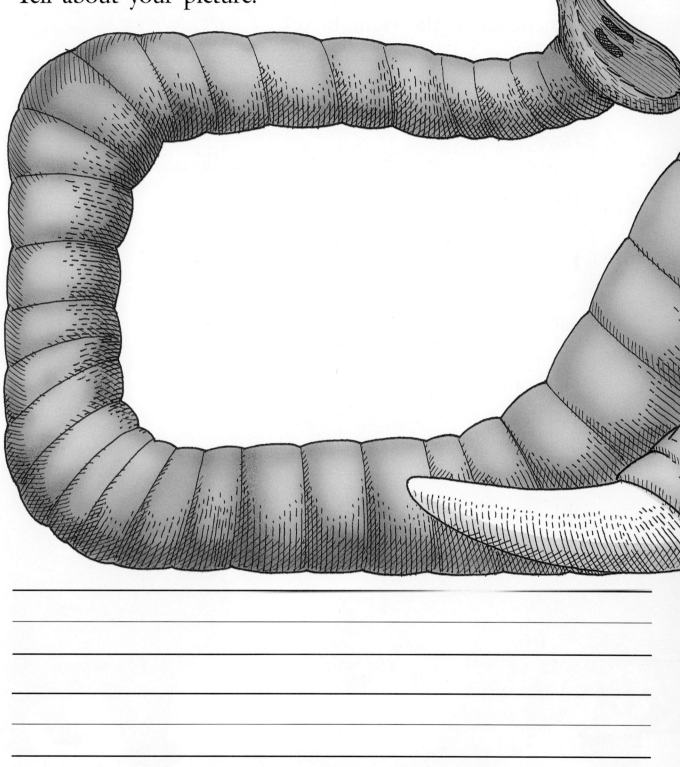

All Kinds of Cats

Think about the stories you've read.
Then put checks in the right boxes.

	pet cats	wild cats
have whiskers		
have soft fur		
have sharp claws		
run and leap		
climb trees		
live with people		
do NOT live with people		

Developing Skills Through Literature

Story Elements

Cut out and color the figures to make stick puppets.

Then use the puppets to tell what happened at the beginning, the middle, and the end of the story. Don't forget to tell how Tiger felt, and why.

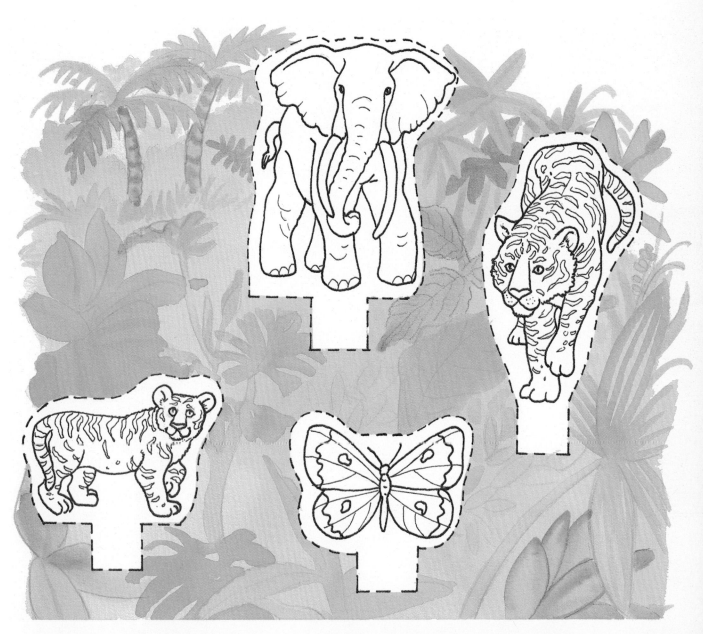

Contractions

Help Tiger tell her mother not to leave her alone.
The two underlined words in each sentence can
be changed to a contraction. Use the words
Tiger is holding to replace the
underlined words.

| There's | I'm | You're | I'd | don't |

_____

<u>You</u> <u>are</u> going hunting again. _____

_____

_____

I <u>do</u> <u>not</u> want to stay here by myself! _____

_____

_____

I <u>am</u> feeling bored. _____

_____

_____

<u>There</u> <u>is</u> no one to play with! _____

_____

_____

<u>I</u> <u>would</u> rather go hunting with you! _____

If you were Tiger, what would you tell your mother?

Exploring and Extending

Animal Babies

Draw a picture of a baby animal.
Then write about it.

Chitina and Her Cat

What are some things that a girl and her cat can do together?
Write two of your ideas here. Then draw a picture of one of them.

_____

_____

1. _____

_____

_____

2. _____

Talk about your ideas with a friend.

Developing Vocabulary

Finish this story. For each sentence, choose one word to complete it. Use what you know about letter sounds and the sense of the sentence to choose the best words.

One night I _____ scared.　　**began**
　　　　　　　　　　　　　　　　　　became

There was no _____ to see by.　　**light**
　　　　　　　　　　　　　　　　　　　coal

Then I _____ to the window.　　**twinkled**
　　　　　　　　　　　　　　　　　　tiptoed

_____

I _____ and watched the stars. **stood**
striped

_____

_____ **curled**

I saw how the moon _____ **beamed**
down at me.

_____

_____

In the morning, the moon _____
and the sun came up. **understood**
disappeared

Trade papers with a friend.
Did you choose the same words?

Chitina and Almost had a nighttime adventure.
Draw a picture of something fun or exciting that
happened to you one night.

Now write about your picture.

_____

_____

_____

_____

_____

Tell a friend about your adventure.

Story Elements

Write what you remember from the story.

▼ **Beginning**

_____

_____

_____

_____

▼ **Middle**

_____

_____

_____

_____

▼ **End**

_____

_____

_____

_____

Comparing Stories

You have read stories about different kinds of cats. Now think about all those stories.

Which stories tell about people and their cats?

- ☐ <u>No One Should Have Six Cats!</u>
- ☐ <u>Tiger Runs</u>
- ☐ <u>Chitina and Her Cat</u>

Which story is about wild animals?

- ☐ <u>No One Should Have Six Cats!</u>
- ☐ <u>Tiger Runs</u>
- ☐ <u>Chitina and Her Cat</u>

Which stories happen around a home?

- ☐ <u>No One Should Have Six Cats!</u>
- ☐ <u>Tiger Runs</u>
- ☐ <u>Chitina and Her Cat</u>

Which story has no people in it?

- ☐ <u>No One Should Have Six Cats!</u>
- ☐ <u>Tiger Runs</u>
- ☐ <u>Chitina and Her Cat</u>

Which story was your favorite? Why?

_____

_____

_____

_____

_____

Short and Long e

Pretend Almost is telling a cat friend what happened to him. Read these sentences with a partner.

One night I couldn't sleep very well.
I went for a walk down the street.
It didn't seem far, but it was.
I heard Chitina yell but I didn't see her.
I followed the sweet smell of the flowers.
It led me back home.

Now make a list of all the short e words.
Make another list of all the long e words.

Short e Words	Long e Words

Name That Pet

Chitina named her cat "Almost" because he was almost as black as coal and almost as striped as a tiger. Can you find names to fit each animal below?

_____

_____

_____

_____

_____

_____

Change papers with a friend. Do you like the names your friend picked?

A Theme PROJECT

Have a Class Cat Show

Choosing and Planning

The stories in "Cats" are about many kinds of cats. Fill your room with cats! Have a class cat show.

- Pick a cat to find out about.
- Find out about that cat.
- Make a cat to bring to the show.
- Plan your show.
- Get your show ready.

What kinds of cats do you know about? Here are some. Do you know about others?

Persian

Lynx

Cheetah

Lion

Panther

Siamese

Bobcat

Can you find pictures of more cats?

Ask your teacher for help.

Go to the library. Ask to see pictures of cats. Find out about cats that are pets and wild animals.

- Look for books about cats.
- Look for the <u>C</u> encyclopedia.

What cats do you want to find out about?

An encyclopedia has lots of facts and pictures. The <u>C</u> book has a part called Cats.

Write their names.

_____

_____

_____

_____

_____

Which cat will you make? Circle it.

CAT

Now think about this.
How will you make your cat?

☐ I will draw or paint it.

☐ I will use clay.

☐ I will cut it out of paper.

☐ I will make a mask.

_____

_____

☐ My idea _____ .

Do you know what you want to do?
Finish these sentences.

Checkpoint

_____

_____

The cat I picked is a _____ .

_____

_____

To show my cat, I'll make a _____

_____

_____

_____ .

Putting It Together

Copy a picture of your cat.

Find out about your cat. Then finish the card below.

Cat Card

_____

_____

My name is _____.

_____

My kind of cat is _____.

_____

This cat lives in _____.

_____

This cat can _____.

- What do you need to make your cat?
  Be sure you have everything before you start.

- Make your cat.

- Then make a neat copy of your Cat Card.

Presenting the Project

What will you do at your show?
Here are two ideas.

- Have a cat contest. Ask
  visitors to vote.

- Make cat noises into a tape
  recorder. Purr or meow.
  Roar like a lion.

Who will come to your show?

- Will other classes come?
  Make a poster to tell them
  about the show.

- Will friends and family
  come? Send them invitations.

VOTE	
Scariest	_____
Prettiest	_____
Strangest	_____
Fluffiest	_____
Funniest	_____
Smallest	_____
Biggest	_____
Friendliest	_____

Checkpoint

Who will come
to our show? _____

_____

_____

What will we
do at our show? _____

My Own Project Plan

What can I find out? Here are some ideas.

_____

_____

_____

_____

_____

              _____

              _____

I will learn about _____.

This is how I will find things out.

_____

_____

1. _____

_____

_____

2. _____

_____

_____

3. _____

This is what I will make or do.

Writing Center

Describing Cats

PREWRITING ▶

I Can Write About...
What kind of cat can you write about?
Draw pictures of two cats.

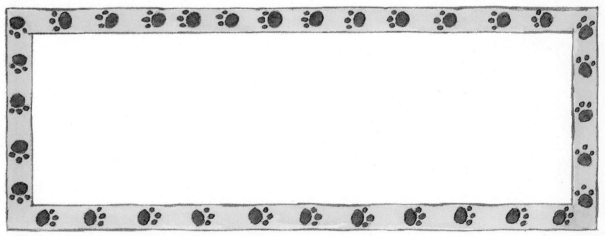

Talk about your pictures with someone.
Choose one to write about.

I Can Tell...

Make a bigger picture of the cat
you want to write about.

What can you tell about your cat?
What does it look like? Where does it live?

Draw a picture to show more about
your cat.

Now tell someone about your cat.

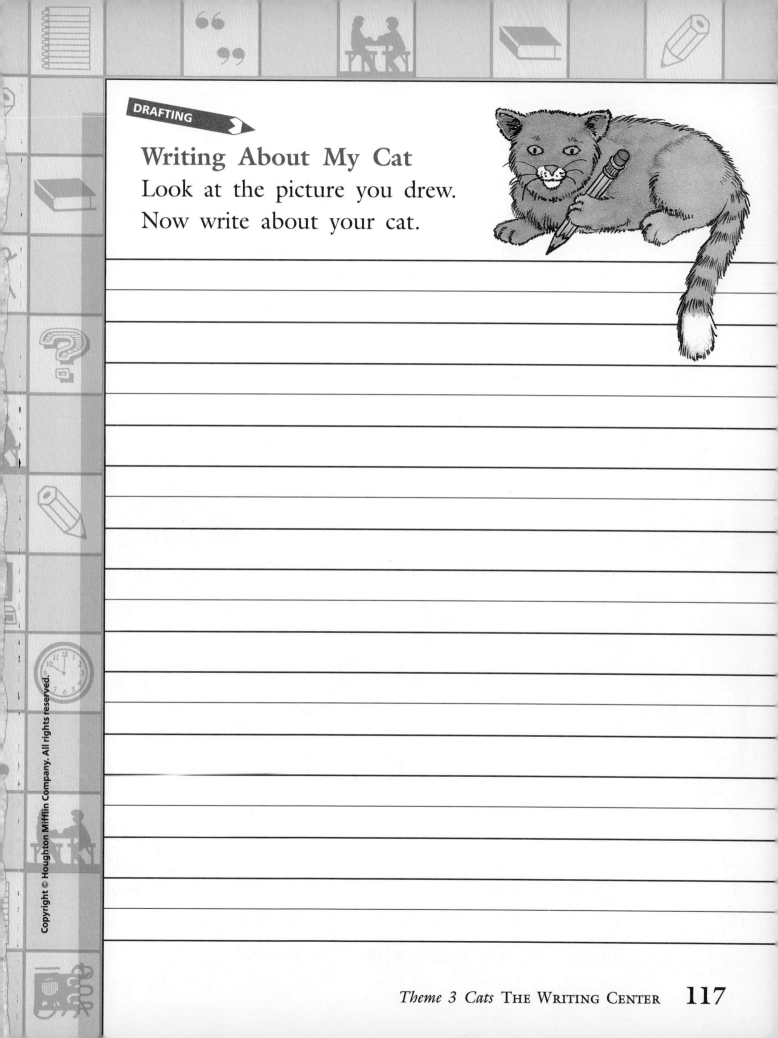

DRAFTING

Writing About My Cat

Look at the picture you drew.
Now write about your cat.

Writing More

Read what you wrote to someone.

Then talk about it.

Here are some things to talk about.

- Can you tell more about your cat?
- What color is it?
- Does it have stripes or spots?
- How does it feel?
- What sound does the cat make?

Read to yourself what you wrote.

What can you add?

Go back and write more.

Sharing Your Final Copy

Think of a title.

Copy what you wrote about your cat.

How can you share what you wrote?

Who Can Fix It?

What do you do when something is broken?
Who fixes it for you?

Finish these pictures. Show who will fix the broken things.

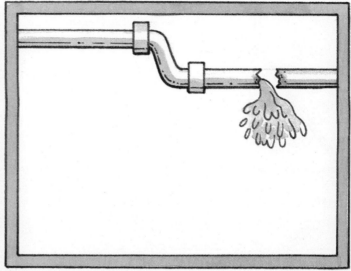

Be ready to tell more about how these people fixed the broken things.

Would you like to be a fix-it worker? Draw tools to fill your own tool box.

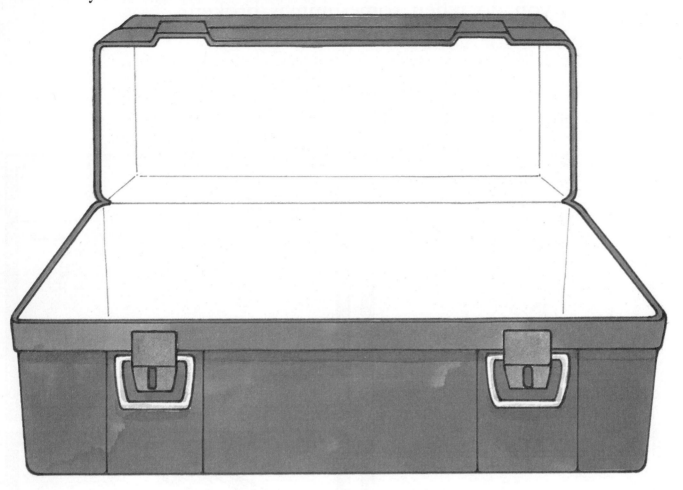

What will you fix with your tools? Write about what you will fix. Then compare your tool box with a friend's.

_____

_____

_____

_____

_____

Social Studies Test

Part A Read the words in the box and the sentences. Decide which word best completes each sentence. Write the word you choose on the lines.

> **tools   plumber   glazier   mechanic**

1. When the car won't start, we need a

    _____

    _____

    _____.

2. When the sink stops up, we need a

    _____

    _____

    _____.

3. When the window gets broken, we need a

    _____

    _____

    _____.

    _____

    _____

4. If I had _____, I could fix almost anything!

Part B Read the sentence. Decide which tool the worker named in the sentence will use. Fill in the circle beside your answer.

1. The <u>plumber</u> will fix the sink.

○ hammer   ○ snake   ○ putty knife

2. The <u>mechanic</u> will fix the car.

○ snake   ○ pliers   ○ putty knife

Part C Read the job named. Then choose the sign that tells about the job. Circle your answer.

Car Mechanic

We Replace
Broken
Windows

We'll Get
You Back
on the Road

Sinks Unclogged
Pipes Tightened

READING ON MY OWN

Name of Book

Name of Book

Name of Book

Name of Book

Name of Book

Name of Book

READING ON MY OWN

Name of Book

Name of Book

Name of Book

Name of Book

Name of Book

Name of Book

Name of Book

Name of Book

Name of Book

Name of Book

Name of Book

Name of Book

READING ON MY OWN

Name of Book

Name of Book

Name of Book

Name of Book

Name of Book

Name of Book

READING ON MY OWN

Name of Book
_____
_____

Name of Book
_____
_____

Name of Book
_____
_____

Name of Book
_____
_____

Name of Book
_____
_____

Name of Book
_____
_____

READING ON MY OWN

Name of Book

_____

_____

Name of Book

_____

_____

Name of Book

_____

_____

Name of Book

_____

_____

Name of Book

_____

_____

Name of Book

_____

_____

STUDENT JOURNAL HANDBOOK

STUDENT JOURNAL HANDBOOK

Contents

READING STRATEGIES

◆ Reading New Words

When you come to a word you cannot read:

> Read to the end
> of the sentence.
> What word would
> <u>make sense</u>?

AND

> Look at the letters
> and think about
> the <u>sounds for</u>
> <u>the letters</u>.

> Try to say the word.
> Does it sound like a real word?

> CHECK:
> Does the word make sense in the sentence?
> Does the word have the right sounds for the letters?

If you still can't read the word, ask for HELP.

Preview and Predict

Preview

1. Read the name of the story.
2. Look at the pictures.
3. Read a little bit of the story.
   What do you know <u>now</u> about the story?

4. What do you think will happen in the story?
5. What do you think you will learn from
   the story?
      Read all of the story.
      Were you right?

Stop and Think

If you are reading a story and it doesn't make sense to you, here's what to do.

1. STOP and THINK about what you have read so far.

2. Look at the pictures and some of the pages you have already read.

3. Read again carefully.

4. Keep reading.
   See if the story begins to make sense.

If you still don't understand, ask for HELP.

Summarizing Stories

Think about the story you just read.

1. WHO were the characters in the story?

2. WHERE did the story take place?

3. What happened <u>first</u>?
   What happened <u>next</u>?
   What happened <u>after that</u>?

4. How did the story END?

5. What did you learn from the story?

If you can't remember parts of the story . . .
   Read some of the story again.
   Talk with someone who has read the story.

THE WRITING PROCESS

 Prewriting

- Talk with your class about special things you have done together.
- Help your teacher list your ideas.
- Talk about each idea.
    - Will it be fun to write about?
    - Do you remember enough about it?
    - Who will your readers be?
    - Will your readers like this idea?
- Choose one idea for a story.

- Talk about what you did first.
- Talk about what you did next.
- Talk about what you did last.

- Draw pictures of what you liked best.

◆2◆ Drafting

- Remember what you talked about.
- Look at your pictures for ideas.
- Help your teacher make sentences to tell the story.

3 ▸ Revising

- Read your class story together.
- Talk about ways to make the story better.
- Tell what to add.

We went to the pond.

We had lunch there.

There were many animals at the pond.

We liked the ducks.

We liked the frogs, too.

We had fun.

4 ◆ **Publishing**

- Help your teacher make a final copy.
- Add a title.
- Add your pictures to the story.
- Think of ways to share your class story.

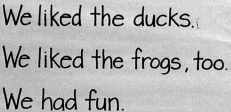

Our Pond Trip
We went to the pond.
We had lunch there.
There were many animals
at the pond.
We liked the ducks.
We liked the frogs, too.
We had fun.

THE SPELLING GUIDE

How to Study a Word

1 LOOK at the word. Name and touch each letter.

2 SAY the word.

3 THINK about the word.

4 WRITE the word.

5 CHECK the spelling.

SPELLING LIST

Do Like Kyla

The Long o Sound

so	home
go	bone

Spelling Words

1. so
2. home
3. go
4. bone
5. no
6. joke

Challenge Words

1. those
2. close

Your Own Words
Add your own spelling words on the back. ⋯⋯>

143

SPELLING LIST

Fix-It

The Short o Sound

got	on	job

Spelling Words

1. got
2. on
3. job
4. lot
5. mop
6. pot

Challenge Words

1. shop
2. rock

Your Own Words
Add your own spelling words on the back. ⋯⋯>

143

SPELLING LIST

This Is the Bear

Words with ot, op, or ox

not	top	box
hot	hop	fox

Spelling Words

1. not
2. top
3. box
4. hop
5. fox
6. hot

Challenge Words

1. stop
2. spot

Your Own Words
Add your own spelling words on the back. ⋯⋯>

143

SPELLING AND WRITING WORD LISTS

Your Own Words

_____
_____

1. _____
_____
_____

2. _____
_____
_____

3. _____
_____
_____

4. _____

Writer's Words from the Story

Learn to spell these words to use in your own writing.

1. is
2. there
3. as

LOOK

SAY

THINK

WRITE

CHECK

144

SPELLING AND WRITING WORD LISTS

Your Own Words

_____
_____

1. _____
_____
_____

2. _____
_____
_____

3. _____
_____
_____

4. _____

Writer's Words from the Story

Learn to spell these words to use in your own writing.

1. out
2. what
3. her

LOOK

SAY

THINK

WRITE

CHECK

144

SPELLING AND WRITING WORD LISTS

Your Own Words

_____
_____

1. _____
_____
_____

2. _____
_____
_____

3. _____
_____
_____

4. _____

Writer's Words from the Story

Learn to spell these words to use in your own writing.

1. do
2. now
3. our

LOOK

SAY

THINK

WRITE

CHECK

144

Strange Bumps

The Long u **Sound**

cute   rule   June

Spelling Words

1. cute
2. rule
3. June
4. cube
5. tune
6. mule

Challenge Words

1. huge
2. flute

Your Own Words
Add your own spelling words on the back. ·····>

145

The Gunnywolf

The Short u Sound

up   just   sun

Spelling Words

1. up
2. just
3. sun
4. bug
5. cup
6. must

Challenge Words

1. jump
2. duck

Your Own Words
Add your own spelling words on the back. ·····>

145

Klippity Klop

Words with ut, us, **or** un

but   us   fun
cut   bus   run

Spelling Words

1. but
2. us
3. fun
4. bus
5. run
6. cut

Challenge Words

1. shut
2. plus

Your Own Words
Add your own spelling words on the back. ·····>

145

Your Own Words

1. _____

2. _____

3. _____

4. _____

Writer's Words from the Story

Learn to spell these words to use in your own writing.

1. into
2. over
3. down

LOOK

SAY

THINK

WRITE

CHECK

Your Own Words

1. _____

2. _____

3. _____

4. _____

Writer's Words from the Story

Learn to spell these words to use in your own writing.

1. about
2. could
3. back

LOOK

SAY

THINK

WRITE

CHECK

Your Own Words

1. _____

2. _____

3. _____

4. _____

Writer's Words from the Story

Learn to spell these words to use in your own writing.

1. are
2. were
3. would

LOOK

SAY

THINK

WRITE

CHECK

Chitina and Her Cat

The Long e Sound

be	see
he	sleep

Spelling Words

1. be
2. see
3. he
4. she
5. we
6. sleep

Challenge Words

1. free
2. sweet

Your Own Words
Add your own spelling words on the back. ----->

147

Tiger Runs

The Short e Sound

get	red	then

Spelling Words

1. get
2. red
3. then
4. yes
5. them
6. best

Challenge Words

1. help
2. next

Your Own Words
Add your own spelling words on the back. ----->

147

No One Should Have Six Cats!

Words with et, ed, or en

pet	fed	men
let	bed	ten

Spelling Words

1. pet
2. fed
3. let
4. bed
5. men
6. ten

Challenge Words

1. sled
2. shed

Your Own Words
Add your own spelling words on the back. ----->

147

SPELLING AND WRITING WORD LISTS

Your Own Words

_____

1. _____

_____

2. _____

_____

3. _____

_____

4. _____

Writer's Words from the Story

Learn to spell these words to use in your own writing.

1. other
2. has
3. two

LOOK
SAY
THINK
WRITE
CHECK

SPELLING AND WRITING WORD LISTS

Your Own Words

_____

1. _____

_____

2. _____

_____

3. _____

_____

4. _____

Writer's Words from the Story

Learn to spell these words to use in your own writing.

1. very
2. after
3. more

LOOK
SAY
THINK
WRITE
CHECK

SPELLING AND WRITING WORD LISTS

Your Own Words

_____

1. _____

_____

2. _____

_____

3. _____

_____

4. _____

Writer's Words from the Story

Learn to spell these words to use in your own writing.

1. your
2. their
3. little

LOOK
SAY
THINK
WRITE
CHECK